Learning Language Arts through Literature

THE GREEN BOOK

By

Diane Welch and Susan Simpson

Common Sense Press

Learning Language Arts through Literture Series

The Blue Book - 1st Grade Skills
The Red Book - 2nd Grade Skills
The Yellow Book - 3rd Grade Skills
The Orange Book - 4th - 5th Grade Skills
The Purple Book - 5th - 6th Grade Skills
The Tan Book - 6th Grade Skills
The Green Book - 7th - 8th Grade Skills
The Gray Book - 8th - 9th Grade Skills
The Gold Book - High School Skills

Copyright, 1992

Common Sense Press
P.O. Box 1365
8786 Highway 21
Melrose, FL 32666
(904) 475-5757

Printed in the United States of America

ISBN 1-880892-34-0

Introduction

As parents we watched and marveled at the way our little ones learned to talk. By listening and responding to English spoken well, they were able to communicate quite clearly. The process was so gradual that they were not even aware it was taking place.

It is the belief of those associated with the *Learning Language Arts Through Literature* series that written language can best be learned in the same manner. By reading fine literature and working with good models of writing, students will receive a quality education in language arts. If you desire to teach using this integrated approach to language, this curriculum is for you.

In her books, Dr. Ruth Beechick has confirmed that this method of teaching is an appropriate and successful way to introduce our students to the joys of reading, writing and thinking. Our own experiences using these lessons with children have encouraged us to share them with you. Their enjoyment and enthusiasm for reading and writing is an unmatched recommendation for this method of teaching.

How To Use This Book

This book will help you teach your child language arts skills. It provides you with materials and suggestions that will be an encouragement and benefit to you as you create a learning environment for your family.

The Green Book is intended for use between the Tan Book and Gray Book of the *Learning Language Arts Through Literature* series. The Tan Book and the Gray Book are based on dictation lessons, while the Green Book utilizes a unit study approach to language arts. This is intended to give the student a change of pace and help you, the teacher, explore new activities to encourage excitement in your child's writing assignments. As in the other books in this series, we have made an effort to use fine literature whenever possible to serve as a model for your child.

The Green Book is divided into seven units. You may choose to teach the units in any order that fits your schedule. The seven units are:

Parts of the Sentence/Sentence Diagramming (six weeks) - The student will have a thorough review of the parts of sentences and learn how to diagram them in order to strengthen his understanding of how these parts fit together. Sentences to be worked with have been adapted from works of fine literature.

Poetry (six weeks) - The student will enjoy reading, memorizing, analyzing, and writing poetry.

Writing A Research Paper (three weeks) - The student will learn the research process in manageable steps.

Speech (three weeks) - The student will prepare and present an oral presentation.

The Short Story (six weeks) - This unit is divided into three 2-week sessions. The student will learn the four general steps to develop the plot of a story and write three short stories in suggested settings.

The Star of Light (four weeks) - While reading this book the student will complete such assignments as writing character sketches, comparing and contrasting cultures and religions, drawing maps, narrating, and more.

Adam and His Kin (four weeks) - A narrative history of the first eleven chapters of Genesis by Dr. Ruth Beechick is the basis for this four-week unit. The student will develop skills in researching, drawing graphs, and writing narration.

In addition to the units, you can help improve your student's spelling and vocabulary by using the following weekly schedule:

DAY 1:   Form the list. The first source of words to be learned should come from the student's writing. He should be writing something each week, either from the above lessons or from letters, journals, stories, or other papers assigned. He needs to learn to spell the words he uses. Another important source should be taken from his lessons in reading, history, science, Bible, etc. For example, if you are beginning a lesson in science or a geography chapter, pull any words you feel he needs to know from the lesson before you begin. As he studies these words, it will help him to understand the lesson much better as it increases their vocabulary. You may also wish to pull a few words from a word list. Ten to fifteen words should be enough.

Dictate the word list to the student. Then go over each word, writing it correctly and underlining the "bear parts". (These are the parts the student misspelled.) For example, if the word <u>abundant</u> were spelled "abundent," the student does not need to concentrate on the first part of the word, he already knows how to spell it. Just point out the <u>ant</u> part and underline the <u>a</u>. It is a good idea to also have the student practice pronouncing the word correctly. Many spelling errors are made because the student is mispronouncing the word.

DAY 2:   Today the student will spend time studying the words by dividing them into syllables and accenting them. Example: a bun' dant. Any words he is not absolutely sure he knows the meaning of should be looked up. Remember, you are trying to expand his vocabulary as well as improve his spelling.

DAY 3:   This is the day the student exhibits how well he understands the meaning of the word and also is an exercise in creative writing. The student will write a sentence for each word (it is permissible to use more than one spelling/vocabulary word in a sentence). The sentences should be well written and should show the student's mastery of the word. Just for fun he could try using the words in a continuing story.

DAY 4:   Private study of the words. The student should say the word, thinking of its spelling, write the word, and then check it with his paper.

DAY 5:   You will dictate sentences you have made up using the spelling words to your student. You may use more than one spelling/vocabulary word in each sentence. Any words misspelled, even if they were not on this week's spelling list, are added to next week's spelling list.

Following the units in this book you will find the **Teacher Helps** for several of the lessons. Next, you will find the **Skills Index**, dividing the skills by by units. A **Bibliography** of books used in the lessons and other helpful books concludes the manual.

PARTS OF SENTENCE/SENTENCE DIAGRAMMING

A Six Week Unit

This unit will help you review the major and minor parts of speech as you study the parts of a sentence. You will also learn how to diagram a sentence as a way of analyzing and understanding how these parts work together.

We believe that sentence diagramming serves two functions for your student's education. First, it functions as a cultural literacy component. Even though sentence diagramming is not done by anyone on a regular basis, it is an abililty that most people in our culture have acquired.

Secondly, for some children, the visual analysis of a sentence will be helpful in learning a second language. Although the sentence structure may vary for this new language, a clear understanding of our terminology and a concept of the parts of speech in our language will help the student comprehend the grammar of the new language.

Having given our reasons for sentence diagramming, let us also encourage you to use this unit in a manner that best suits you and your student. You may want to use two or three lessons, then go to another unit and return for the final three lessons. If your student has difficulty with grammar, you may want to use another unit before this one. Please remember that the units in this book are designed to be used in any order that meets the needs of your school.

LESSON ONE

Day One   **Nouns, Pronouns, and Verbs**

<u>Definitions</u>:

Noun   a word used to name a person, place, thing, or idea. ex: girl, city, book, joy. A proper noun names a particular person, place, thing, or idea and is always capitalized. ex: Mary Jones, Atlanta, <u>A Tale of Two Cities</u>

Pronoun   a word that takes the place of a noun. ex: he, her, you, it

Verb   a word that expresses action or states a condition of being. ex: Action - run, laugh, trust; Being - am, are, is, was, were, be, been, being

A complete sentence has two important parts: a subject and a predicate. The subject is the part about which something is being said and is usually a noun or pronoun. The predicate is the part that tells something about the subject and contains the verb. When trying to label the parts of a sentence, it is usually easier to locate the verb first. A simple way of doing this is to see if the verb sounds right in the following blanks:

He _____s.   He is _____ing.

(Note: State of being verbs require some changes to fit the blanks. ex: She is happy. She is being happy.)

Once you have found the verb, put the words <u>who</u> or <u>what</u> in front of the verb.

Locate the verb and the subject of the verb in the following passage:

The rest of our journey was very easy. A little after sunset we reached the house of my master's friend. We were taken into a clean, snug stable. A kind coachman made us very comfortable.

(<u>Black Beauty</u> by Anna Sewell)

Review the parts of sentences learned yesterday. Spend a few minutes finding these parts using books in your home.

Diagramming:

Since the foundation of a sentence is the simple verb and simple subject of the verb, we will always start our diagramming with these two sentence parts as follows:

The sentence "The rest of our journey was very easy" would look like this:

Diagram the other sentences in yesterday's exercise. You will not be diagramming every word, just the simple verb and simple subject of the verb.

Day Three   **Adjectives**

Definition:

Adjectives   a word that modifies (changes the meaning of something in such a way as to limit it or make it more specific) a noun or a pronoun. Adjectives answer the questions <u>What kind?</u> <u>How many or how much?</u> or <u>Which one</u>?

ex: <u>heavy</u> rock, <u>two</u> books, <u>first</u> girl

Most adjectives can be compared using -er, -est, or more, most.

A simple test for adjectives:

The _____ thing (or person) is very _____.

Adjectives can fill both of these blanks. ex: The heavy thing is very heavy.

Determiners   a word that signals that a noun is coming.
    1.   articles - a, an, the
    2.   possessives - my, our, your, his, her, its, their, Joe's

Locate the adjectives in the following passage and tell what noun they modify:

A huge tawny mastiff lay on the floor. This great creature rose majestically. The little fellow watched him approach.

(<u>Little Lord Fauntleroy</u> by Francis Hodgson Burnett)

Day Four   **Diagramming Adjectives**

Review the definitions of adjectives and determiners. Using books in your home, locate these parts of speech.

Diagramming: Adjectives are diagramed on an angled line attached to the base line below the word modified.

We will diagram the subject, verb, and adjectives using yesterday's passage:

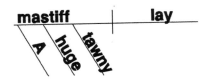

Continue diagramming the sentences. (Note: Again you will not be diagramming each word.)

Day Five Review Nouns, Pronouns, Verbs, Adjectives, and Determiners

You may continue pulling sentences out of books to diagram, OR
Write your own and diagram, OR
You may spend time writing descriptive sentences, OR
Write a paragraph concentrating on using these parts of speech.

LESSON TWO

Definition - words that modify verbs, adjectives, or other adverbs. They answer the questions <u>How</u>? <u>When</u>? <u>Where</u>? and <u>To what extent or degree</u>?

ex: The rabbit moved <u>quickly</u>. (How)
She will arrive <u>soon</u>. (When)
I went <u>there</u>. (Where)
His hands plunged <u>deeply</u> into the snow. (To what extent)

(Note: <u>Not</u> is an adverb that does not fit the three meanings. It is used to make a sentence negative.)

While adjectives usually appear just before the noun that they modify, adverbs usually do not appear just before the verbs that they modify. Adverbs often appear after the verb or after the direct object, if there is one; but it may appear between a helping verb and the verb. Sometimes they even appear before the complete verb or even before the subject, at the beginning of the sentence.

ex: I will go home <u>now</u>.
I will <u>now</u> go home.
I <u>now</u> will go home.
<u>Now</u> I will go home.

Locate the adverbs in the following passage and tell what verb they modify:

The engine itself almost seemed to hear her. She saw the great black engine stop. Bobbie could not stop waving the flag. She waved it feebly. Then she fainted.
(<u>The Railway Children</u> by E. Nesbit)

Review the definition of adverbs, and locate examples in books of your choosing.

Diagramming - Adverbs are diagrammed on an angled line attached to the base line below the word modified.

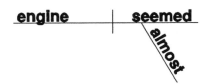

Diagram the last three sentences in yesterday's passage.

Day Three   **Direct Objects and Indirect Objects**

Definitions:

Direct Object   a noun or pronoun that follows an action verb and receives the action of the verb. It answers the questions <u>whom</u> or <u>what</u> after the verb.
ex: John built the <u>doghouse</u>.

Indirect Object   a noun or pronoun that answers the question <u>to whom</u> or <u>for whom</u> after the verb. It always comes between the verb and the direct object. It never follows the preposition <u>to</u> or <u>for</u>.
Note: If there is **no** direct object, there will be **no** indirect object.

Locate the direct objects in the following passage:

His doctor advised him to take horse exercise. For this purpose he bought me. He hired a stable a short distance from his lodgings. He engaged a man named Fletcher as groom.

(<u>Black Beauty</u> by Anna Sewell)

Locate the indirect object in the following sentence, also from <u>Black Beauty</u>:

One cold windy day, Dolly had brought Jerry a basin of something hot.

Day Four   Diagramming Direct Objects and Indirect Objects

Review the parts of sentences learned yesterday. Spend a few minutes finding these parts using books in your home.

Diagramming:

First diagram the subject and the verb. After the verb draw a vertical line that does not cross the base line and add the simple direct object to the right of the new line. If there is an indirect object, add a slanted line below the verb line with a line attached to it running parallel to the base line. The indirect object is written on the line parallel to the base line.

Diagram yesterday's sentences.

1.   Locate and diagram sentences containing adverbs, direct objects, and indirect objects. Or

2.   Write your own sentences and diagram them. Or

3.   Write a narrative paragraph containing these parts of sentences.

LESSON THREE

Day One   **Predicate Adjectives and Predicate Nouns**

<u>Definitions</u>:

Predicate Adjective   follows the verb and describes the subject.
ex: Her eyes are <u>green</u>.

Predicate Noun   follows the verb and renames the subject.
ex: Jesus is the <u>Son</u> of <u>God</u>.

Locate the predicate adjectives and predicate nouns in the following passage:

> My new master's name was Jeremiah Barker. His wife was a good match for him. She was plump. The boy was tall. He was a good tempered lad.

(<u>Black Beauty</u> by Anna Sewell)

Day Two   **Diagramming Predicate Adjectives and Predicate Nouns**

Review the definitions of predicate adjectives and predicate nouns. Using books in your home, locate examples of these parts of sentences.

Diagramming: Predicate adjectives and predicate nouns are diagrammed in the same way. Add a slanted line to the base line between the verb and either the predicate adjective or predicate noun.

```
  name    |  was   \  Jeremiah Barker
_____|_____
          |
```

Continue diagramming yesterday's sentences.

Definition:

Qualifiers   words that modify adjectives and adverbs. Qualifiers are used to strengthen or weaken the idea of the adjective or adverb.
ex: The peach pie tasted <u>really</u> good.

Locate the qualifiers in the following passage:

She happened quite accidentally. **We were not looking very earnestly** for a Princess. Noel had said he was going to marry a Princess. He really did so. **It was rather odd.** When people say things are going to befall, **very often they don't. It was somewhat different,** of course, with the prophets of old.

(<u>The Treasure Seekers</u> by E. Nesbit)

Review the definition of qualifiers. Locate examples in books.

Diagramming:

When the qualifier modifies a regular adjective or adverb, draw a horizontal line to the line of the adjective or adverb and attach a line parallel to the line of the adjective or adverb for the qualifier. As follows:

Diagram the bold sections from yesterday's sentences.

Day Five Review Predicate Adjectives, Predicate Nouns, and Qualifiers

1.   Continue practicing diagramming predicate adjectives, predicate nouns, and qualifiers by using sentences located in your own books. Or
2.   Write your own sentences using these parts of sentences. Or
3.   Write a paragraph describing a person or place using these parts of sentences.

LESSON FOUR

Day One   **Prepositional Phrases Part One**

<u>Definitions</u>:

Preposition   a word that shows a connection between a noun or a pronoun (object of the preposition) and some other word in the sentence. A word has to have an object to be a preposition.
Some common prepositions:
    at, by, for, from, in, of, on, to, with

Prepositional
Phrase   made up of a preposition and a noun phrase. The main noun or pronoun in the noun phrase is the simple object of the preposition.

ex: The cat was <u>on</u> <u>our</u> <u>roof</u>.

Locate the prepositional phrases in the following passages:

Joe put Merrylegs into the mistress' low chaise. He said goodbye to us. Merrylegs neighed to us. John put the saddle on Ginger. He rode us across the country.

(<u>Black Beauty</u> by Anna Sewell)

Day Two   **Prepositional Phrases Part Two**

Prepositional phrases that modify nouns do the job of an adjective. If they modify the verb then they do the job of an adverb.

Locate the prepositional phrases in the following passage and tell whether they are adjectival prepositional phrases or adverbial prepositional phrases.

Katy was at her wits' end. They scarcely ever went into the parlor. Aunt Issie regarded it as a sort of sacred place. She kept petticoats over all the chairs. She never opened the blinds for fear of flies.

(<u>What Katy Did</u> by Susan Coolidge)

Day Three   Diagramming Prepositional Phrases

Write the preposition on a slanted line below the word modified. The object of the preposition is written on a line attached to the slanted line and running parallel to the base line. The modifiers of the object of the preposition are added below it.

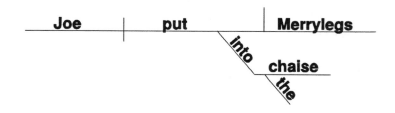

Diagram the sentences from the paragraph on Day One.

Day Four   Reviewing Prepositional Phrases

Choose a book from your library and find twenty prepositional phrases. Make a list of the different prepositions you find.

Definition:

Interjections   words showing strong feelings that either stand alone, punctuated as a sentence; or that appear in a regular sentence and set apart by a comma.

ex: <u>Oh</u>! He fell in!
      <u>Well</u>, I wouldn't have believed it!

Locate the interjections in the following sentences:

Oh, I see.

Yes, I would like a dog.

Right, we will be home at 4:00.

Please, shut the door.

Sure, you can go.

Hello! I am Ann Smith.

Diagramming:

Diagram the basic parts of the sentence and then add the interjection on a separate line just above the left end of the diagram.

Diagram the sentences listed above.

LESSON FIVE

Day One   **Conjunctions**

<u>Definition</u>:

Conjunctions   a connecting word that joins words or groups of words in a sentence.

ex: and, but, or

Conjunctions may join single words:

ex: Tom **and** Jim sang a duet.

or phrases:

ex: Sharon bought the red plaid skirt **and** the blue skirt.

or two complete sentences:

ex: I had a sandwich for lunch **and** my sister had pizza.

This week you will learn the different ways to diagram compound parts.

Compound Subject:

Split the subject line into two lines and join the two lines with a broken line. The conjunction is written on the broken line.

Compound Verb:

Split the verb line into two lines and join the two lines with a broken line.
The conjunction is written on the broken line.

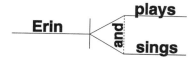

Diagram the sentences in this passage:

Bobbie clutched the parcel tighter and bent her head over it. She
went on tiptoe to her room and locked the door. Then she undid the
parcel and read that printed column again. Her hands and feet were icy
cold.

(The Railway Children by E. Nesbit)

Compound Modifiers, Compound Object of the Preposition
Day Two   **Compound Direct Objects**

Diagramming Compound Modifiers:

Join the two slanted lines with a broken line and write the conjunction on the
broken line.

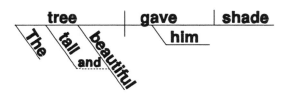

23

Diagramming Compound Object of a Preposition:

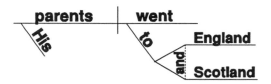

Diagramming Compound Direct Objects:

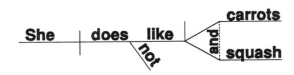

Diagram the sentences in this passage:

The large and beautiful room was impressive. The furniture was not massive and antique. The draperies and rugs were brighter. Shelves were full of books and toys. His grandfather had provided the books and playthings for his amusement.

(Little Lord Fauntleroy by Francis Hodgson Burnett)

Day Three   Compound Phrases

Compound phrases are diagrammed like compound words. Any related words and modifiers are added as usual. The sentences today are taken from Rebecca of Sunnybrook Farm by Kate Douglas Wiggin.

Compound Complete Subject:

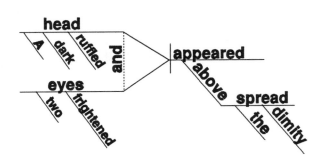

Compound Complete Predicate:

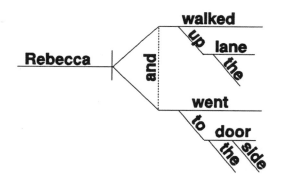

Compound prepositional phrases:

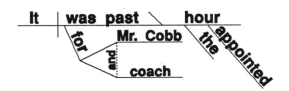

Diagram the following sentences:

He put the whip in its socket and took his foot from the dashboard.

She put a vase of apple blossoms and a red tomato pincushion on Rebecca's bureau.

The window looked out on the back buildings and the barn.

Rebecca stood perfectly still in the center of the room and looked about her.

The last glimpse of the routed Simpson tribe and the last flutter of their tattered garments disappeared in the dim distance.

Day Four   **Compound Sentences**

Each independent clause has a base line. The second clause is directly below the first clause and the conjunction is on a solid line between the two verbs. The broken vertical lines are drawn to each other.

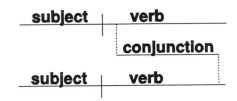

Diagram the sentences in the following passage:

The little schoolhouse on the hill had its moments of triumph, but it was fortunate that Rebecca had her books to keep her interested. Her new acquaintances kept her interested or life would have gone heavily with her. She tried to like Aunt Mirando but she failed ignominiously in the attempt. She was a faulty child, but she had a sense of duty.

(<u>Rebecca of Sunnybrook Farm</u> by Kate Douglas Wiggin)

Day Five

Since you have had a lot of diagramming to do this week, spend today's time writing or reading anything you please.

LESSON SIX

Day One _____ **Gerunds and Gerund Phrases**

Definitions:

Gerund   A gerund is the -<u>ing</u> form of a verb that is used as a noun.
ex: <u>Reading</u> is my favorite pastime.

Since a gerund acts as a noun, it can be used as a subject (as in the above example), a direct or indirect object, an object of a preposition, or a predicate noun.

**Gerund
Phrase**   consists of a gerund and any modifiers or complements connected with the gerund. A gerund phrase always functions as a noun in a sentence:
ex: We tried <u>fixing the flat tire</u>.

Gerund phrases, like single-word gerunds, function as nouns do.

Locate the gerund or gerund phrase in the following verses taken from Proverbs (NASV):

Blessings are on the head of the righteous. (10:6)

Keeping away from strife is an honor for a man. (20:2)

The getting of treasures by a lying tongue is a fleeting vapor. (21:6)

The churning of milk produces butter. (30:33)

The churning of anger produces strife. (30:33)

The teaching of kindness is on her tongue. (31:26)

Incline your heart to understanding. (2:3)

My son, do not forget my teaching. (3:l)

Day Two   **Participles and Participial Phrases**

Definitions:

Participle   a verb form that is used as an adjective.
                        ex: The <u>dripping</u> faucet kept us awake.

                        A participle is either of two principal parts of a verb - the
                        present participle form (the -<u>ing</u> form of a verb) or the past
                        participle form (the -<u>ed</u> form of a regular verb or irregular
                        verbs formed in various ways).

**Participial
Phrase**   consists of a participle and any modifiers or complements
                        connected with that participle. A participial phrase always
                        functions as an adjective in a sentence.
                        ex: <u>Feeling confident</u>, Mary continued her recitation.

Locate the participle or participial phrase in the following sentences from <u>The Swiss Family Robinson</u>:

My weeping wife looked bravely up.

She began to cheer and encourage them with loving words.

The roaring waters poured in on all sides.

Ernest enjoyed the thought of drinking the refreshing milk.

We can bring damaged biscuits from the wreck.

We commended ourselves to His loving care.

A great rushing noise terrified us dreadfully.

We observed broken eggshells at no great distance.

Day Three   Infinitives and Infinitive Phrases

Definition:

Infinitives   made up usually of <u>to</u> and the first principal part of the verb.
                        ex: We want <u>to win</u>.

**Infinitive
Phrases**   a group of related words consisting of an infinitive, its
                        modifiers, complements, and/or subject that function as a single
                        noun or modifier.
                        ex: He decided <u>to run in the race</u>.

Locate the infinitive or infinitive phrase in the following sentences from <u>The Swiss Family Robinson</u>:

I found it no easy matter to keep my countenance.

It seemed wasteful to cook so many at once.

I had advised her to preserve them.

I promised to go for her cask after dinner.

We began at once to load.

We were ready to leave.

Label each word in the following passage. You may use the following abbreviations: (Subject = subj.; Verb = vb.; Adjective = adj.; Adverb = adv.; Preposition = prep.; Object of the Preposition = o.p.; Gerund = ger.; Conjunction = conj.; Direct Object = D.O.; Infinitive = inf.; Participle = part.)

Turning up his little wrinkled face, Jocko began to grimace and beg for something. The man pulled the string and struck up a merry tune. In a minute the monkey spun around and around at a lively pace and put in many queer antics. The little audience was fairly convulsed with laughter.

(adapted from Five Little Peppers and How They Grew by Margaret Sidney)

Being able to diagram sentences does not make you a better writer. Only actually writing can do that. Diagramming sentences helps you see the relationship between the parts of the sentence. You have also had a good review of the parts of sentences using sentence diagramming to reinforce what you have learned.

You have probably discovered some sentences that you are still not sure how to diagram. When you run into these just diagram the parts you are sure about. At a later date you may wish to pursue a higher study of grammar. Sentence diagramming can be very complicated and a fun challenge.

Find three sentences in a book on your shelf and diagram them.

POETRY

Six-Week Unit

Poetry is an important part of your curriculum. Exploring poetry can increase your fluency and sensitivity to language in all your writing. You will develop self-confidence in writing and develop valuable problem solving skills as you explore figurative language and become aware of new relationships between people, things, and ideas.

Many of us are somewhat afraid of poetry, feeling we just don't understand much of it. Take time during the next six weeks to read poetry aloud to each other, choosing poems that you understand and enjoy. You will "catch" each others' excitement as you share these favorites. Most Fridays you will have the option to hear recitations. Encourage each other to have something memorized to recite. If you do not already have some books of poetry, go to the library and check out several to use during the following weeks.

LESSON ONE
Poetry Appreciation

Day One

Begin looking through the books of poetry you have collected. Enjoy reading aloud poems you like. Do you find a certain poet who is a favorite?

Day Two

As you continue reading poetry aloud, choose a favorite to begin memorizing. Be ready to recite it on Friday.

Day Three

Continue reading poetry aloud. Spend some time memorizing. If you have found a poet to be a favorite, learn something about his or her life.

Day Four

Continue reading poetry aloud and memorizing. Practice reciting your poem using good expression.

Day Five

Recitation Day. Speak clearly and slowly. No gum chewing allowed. Use good expression. Begin by stating the title and author of your poem.

LESSON TWO
Imagery

Day One

Imagery is the use of vivid description to appeal to the reader's sense of sight, hearing, smell, taste, or touch. The pictures or sensations produced in the reader's mind are images of the real thing. The reader's imagination enables him to form these images in his mind.

Writers use figurative language in order to accomplish this imaging. We are going to focus on three types of figurative language - simile, metaphor, and personification.

A simile gives an idea or image of something by comparing it to something else using the connecting word like or as.

ex: The tear down childhood's cheek that flows
            Is like the dew-drop on the rose;
        When next the summer breeze comes by
            And waves the bush, the flower is dry.
                    (Sir Walter Scott)

simile: The tear is like the dew-drop.

Find the simile in this poem:

        A cat sat quaintly by the fire
            And watched the burning coals
        And watched the little flames aspire
            Like small decrepit souls.
                    (From "Hearth" by Peggy Bacon)

Write a sentence that names the two things compared and explain how they are similar.

34

Today you will do some activities that will help you practice comparing things.

Write simile sentence clues for the following objects without naming the object:

Apple
Pencil
Shoe
Marshmallow
Glue

Your clues can describe the size, color, shape, smell, taste, weight, sound, or touch of the object. Try to write more than one clue for each object.

ex: Apple

size: I'm as big as a croquet ball.
color: I'm as red as a rose.
etc.

You can also find similes to make your verbs more expressive.

ex: The sailboats bobbed on the lake like bottle corks.

You try these:

The rain _____ the roof like _____.
The wind _____ in the trees like _____.
The cat _____ on the fence like _____.
The light _____ on the water like _____.

35

Many similes that first come to mind are common sayings we hear quite often. For example, have you ever heard or said "He's as brave as a lion" or "She's as quiet as a mouse"? These are called <u>cliches</u>. A cliche is an overused expression or image. Using the following list of adjectives, write a common expression for each one, then try to write a fresh, new simile for each.

soft as _____

cute as _____

cold as _____

brave as _____

white as _____

If you have time, spend the rest of this period observing the figurative language in your book of poems.

Day Three

Yesterday you did some activities with similes. Today you will practice writing metaphor and personification.

A <u>metaphor</u> is a comparison in which one thing is said to be another:

ex: My bed is a little boat;
                Nurse helps me in when I embark
        She girds me in my sailor's coat
                And starts me in the dark.
            (From "My Bed is a Boat" by Robert Louis Stevenson)

metaphor: My bed is a little boat.

An <u>implied</u> <u>metaphor</u> is a comparison that doesn't use the word <u>like</u> or <u>as</u> or the verb <u>to be</u>.

ex: The Lord proclaims his grace abroad;
       Behold, I change your hearts of stone;
       Each shall renounce his idol god,
       And serve, henceforth, the Lord alone.

       My grace, a flowing stream, proceeds
       To wash your filthiness away;
       Ye shall abhor your former deeds,
       And learn my statutes to obey.
                           (From "The Covenant" by William Cowper)

implied metaphors: hearts of stone
                     My grace, a flowing stream

Find the metaphor in this poem:

       Grace is a plant, where'er it grows,
           Of pure and heav'nly root;
       But fairest in the youngest shews,
           And yields the sweetest fruit.
              (From "Prayer for a Blessing" by William Cowper)

Write a sentence that names the two things compared and explain how they are similar.

We sometimes confuse simile and metaphor. The following example illustrates how we can write a basic comparison and express it as a simile, a metaphor, or an implied metaphor.

ex: Your word is like a lamp unto my feet. (simile)
     Your word is a lamp unto my feet. (metaphor)
     The lamp of your word lights my path. (implied metaphor)

Write the following simile as a metaphor and an implied metaphor and label each appropriately:

Her heart is like a garden, old fashioned, quaint, and sweet.

Using your work from yesterday, rewrite some of your similes as complete sentences, and then write them again as metaphor or implied metaphor.

Personification is a figure of speech in which an animal or inanimate object is given human characteristics.

ex: Out of the bosom of the air,
            Out of the cloud-folds of her garment shaken,
        Over the woodlands brown and bare,
            Over the harvest-fields forsaken,
        Silent, and soft, and slow
            Descends the snow.

personification: Out of the bosom of the air,
                        Out of the cloud-folds of her garment shaken,

Personification is comparing an object to a living thing. The writer is not saying "This is like this" but instead "This behaves like a person".

ex: The wind <u>muttered</u> through the quiet oaks.

Find an example of personification in Emily Dickinson's poem "Autumn":

The morns are meeker than they were,
The nuts getting brown;
The berry's cheek is plumper,
The rose is out of town.

The maple wears a gayer scarf,
The field a scarlet gown.
Lest I should be old-fashioned,
I'll put a trinket on.

Look at the following statements:

The stairs <u>made noise</u>.
A sparrow <u>flew by</u>.
The pencil <u>fell</u> to the floor.
The light <u>came</u> through the trees.

Pretend that each of these things moves or talks or acts like a person. Change the underlined words that show the object acting like a person.

ex: The stairs <u>groaned</u>.

Find examples of a metaphor and personification in your poetry reading today.

Day Four   Free Verse

Most of the poetry you have been reading probably rhymed. The poems you write today and tomorrow will not. Concentrate on word images by using simile, metaphor, or personification as studied during the last few days.

Choose one or more of the following "poem starters":

1. Choosing one subject, write a poem that uses similes that appeal to at least three senses.

2. Write a poem from an object's point of view. Show what the object thinks and how it feels.

3. Choose a color and write a poem describing it using a simile and/or a metaphor.

4.   Choose an activity you are familiar with (playing football, sailing, playing a musical instrument, horseback riding, etc.) and write a poem describing how you feel when you are doing the activity.

Day Five

a)   Continue yesterday's assignment by choosing another poem starter, or continue working on the one you started yesterday.

b)   Read and discuss the comparisons you find in your poetry reading.

c)   Recite the poem(s) you have memorized this week.

LESSON THREE
Structural Poems

Day One   **Haiku**

This week you will be learning and using some common poetry forms - haiku, cinquain, diamante, and limerick. These poems conform to a particular pattern that can be copied.

Haiku - This simple Japanese form of poetry consists of three unrhymed lines, usually containing 17 syllables. The first line contains 5 syllables, the second line, 7 syllables and the third line, 5 syllables. The poem usually deals with nature, very often giving some idea of the season and may contain a surprise at the end.

> ex: Snail, my little man,
> Slowly - ah, very slowly,
> Climb up Mount Fuji!

If possible find some examples of haiku to read before writing your own.

Spend the rest of your time today writing haiku.

Day Two   **Cinquain**

This is another poetry form using the following pattern:

1. Write down a noun or any topic in one word.
2. On the line below that write two adjectives, and separate them by a comma.
3. On the third line, write three verbs that tell what the noun or topic, on the first line, does. Separate them by commas.
4. On the fourth line, write a thought about the word you wrote on the first line. This should be a short phrase (4-5 words) expressing a feeling.
5. On the fifth line, repeat the word you wrote on the first line or write down a synonym or some related word.

ex: Caterpillar
       Plump, Fat,
       Creeping, Crawling, Eating
       Spins a little cocoon
       Butterfly

(Melissa Burger, Age 12)

Write your own cinquain following the rules given above.

Day Three   Diamante

The diamante poetry form derives its name from the diamond shape it creates following the directions below:

1.   Write down a noun (line seven will be an antonym for this word).
2.   On the second line, write two adjectives describing the noun on line one.
3.   On the third line, write three participles ending in -ing describing the word on line one.
4.   On the fourth line, write down two nouns relating to or describing the word on line one and two nouns that relate to or describe the antonym on line seven.
5.   On the fifth line, write three participles ending in -ing that describe the word on line seven.
6.   On the sixth line, write two adjectives describing the word on line seven.
7.   Write an antonym for the word on line one.

ex:

                       Bird
                  Beautiful, Red
             Flying, Singing, Eating
           Clouds, Sky, Paws, Fur
         Running, Jumping, Pouncing
                  Sly, Cautious
                       Cat
(Katherine Welch, Age 12)

Write your own diamante in the shape of a diamond.

The final, and perhaps most familiar poetry form you will use this week is the limerick, a humorous verse of five lines. Read aloud some limericks and listen to the cadence or rhythm of the lines.

Limericks usually follow this pattern:

Lines 1, 2 and 5 rhyme.
Lines 3 and 4 rhyme.
Lines 1, 2, and 5 usually have from 8 to 10 syllables.
Lines 3 and 4 usually have from 5 to 7 syllables.
Typically the first line introduces the character.

> ex: There was a young lady of Niger
>   Who smiled as she rode on a tiger,
>   They returned from the ride
>   With the lady inside,
>   And the smile on the face of the tiger.

Write your own limericks following the above pattern.

Day Five

If you have especially enjoyed any of the structured poems this week, continue writing, or spend some time again reading poetry aloud, or make this a recitation day.

LESSON FOUR
Writing Poetry Using a Model

Day One   **Rhyme Scheme**

Poems that rhyme often follow a consistent scheme or pattern. To identify the scheme we label the ending sounds of each line. Those that rhyme have the same label.

ex: I saw you toss the kites on high	(a)
And blow the birds about the sky;	(a)
And all around I heard you pass,	(b)
Like ladies' skirts across the grass -	(b)
O wind, a-blowing all day long,	(c)
O wind, that sings so loud a song!	(c)
I saw the different things you did,	(d)
But always you yourself you hid.	(d)
I felt you push, I heard you call,	(e)
I could not see yourself at all -	(e)
O wind, a-blowing all day long,	(c)
O wind, that sings so loud a song!	(c)
O you that are so strong and cold,	(f)
O blower, are you young or old?	(f)
Are you a beast of field or tree,	(g)
Or just a stronger child than me?	(g)
O wind, a-blowing all day long,	(c)
O wind, that sings so loud a song!	(c)

(Robert Louis Stevenson)

This poem has a rhyme scheme aabbcc.

The author has freedom to deviate from the rhyme scheme.

ex: The frost is here,   (a)
       And fuel is dear,   (a)
And woods are sear,   (a)
       And fires burn clear,   (a)
And frost is here   (a)
       And has bitten the heel of the going year.   (a)

Bite, frost, bite!   (b)
       You roll up away from the light   (b)
The blue wood-louse, and the plump dormouse,   (c)
       And the bees are still'd, and the flies are kill'd, (d)
And you bite far into the heart of the house,   (c)
       But not into mine.   (e)

Bite, frost, bite!   (b)
       The woods are all the searer,   (f)
The fuel is all the dearer,   (f)
       The fires are all the clearer,   (f)
My spring is all the nearer,   (f)
       You have bitten into the heart of the earth,   (g)
But not into mine.   (e)
("Winter" by Alfred, Lord Tennyson)

Practice identifying the rhyme scheme of some of your favorite poetry.

When listening to poetry we usually hear the syllables of a line in groups of twos or threes. For example, if we stress the first syllable of a word but not the next the rhythm sounds like DUMM-de DUMM-de, etc. We can mark it (/∪). Each of these rhythmic units is called a <u>foot</u>.

There are four basic feet in English verse:

iambic - de-DUMM (∪/)
anapestic - de-de-DUMM (∪∪/)
Trochaic - DUMM-de (/∪)
dactylic - DUMM-de-de (/∪∪)

The number of feet in a line determines its meter:

monometer - one foot	pentameter - five feet
dimeter - two feet	hexameter - six feet
trimeter - three feet	heptameter - seven feet
tetrameter - four feet	octameter - eight feet

To record a description of the rhyme scheme, small numbers that show the number of feet in a line or a group of lines are written after the letters. For example, using Stevenson's poem "The Wind" that we analyzed yesterday, the rhyme scheme was aabbcc. The poem's rhythm is in the iambic foot (unstressed syllable, stressed syllable). There are four feet per line. A full description of its rhyme scheme would be a a b b c c . Feet, meter, and rhyme scheme make up the <u>metrical pattern</u> of the poem.

It is important to remember that poets very often depart from strict metrical patterns. When you scan verses you are just looking for a basic pattern. Also, two readers may scan the same lines in quite different ways.

Scan the following poem and determine its metrical pattern.

See the kitten on the wall,
Sporting with the leaves that fall,
Withered leaves, one, two and three
Falling from the elder tree,
Through the calm and frosty air
Of the morning bright and fair.

See the kitten, how she starts,
Crouches, stretches, paws and darts;
With a tiger-leap half way
Now she meets her coming prey.
Lets it go as fast and then
Has it in her power again.

Now she works with three and four,
Like an Indian conjurer;
Quick as he in feats of art,
Gracefully she plays her part;
Yet were gazing thousands there;
What would little Tabby care?
(William Wordsworth)

47

Analyze the metrical pattern of the following poem.

> The maple is a dainty maid,
>   The pet of all the wood,
> Who lights the dusky forest glade
>   With scarlet cloak and hood.
>
> The elm a lovely lady is,
>   In shimmering robes of gold,
> That catch the sunlight when she moves,
>   And glisten, fold on fold.
>
> The sumac is a gypsy queen,
>   Who flaunts in crimson dressed,
> And wild along the roadside runs,
>   Red blossoms in her breast.
>
> And towering high above the wood,
>   All in his purple cloak,
> A monarch in his splendor is
>   The proud and princely oak.
>   (Anonymous)

Using "Autumn Fancies" as a model, write your own poem about different kinds of flowers, birds, etc. Choose your words carefully.

Analyze the metrical pattern of the first two stanzas of "My Evening Prayer" by Charles H. Gabriel:

> If I have wounded any soul today,
> If I have caused one foot to go astray,
> If I have walked in my own wilful way -
>   Good Lord, forgive!
>
> If I have uttered idle words or vain,
> If I have turned aside from want or pain,
> Lest I myself should suffer through the strain -
>   Good Lord, forgive!

Try modeling another stanza of this poem.

Day Five

Choose another poem to model, or write another verse to an existing poem, or make today a recitation day.

LESSON FIVE
Psalms

Day One

___

We find some of the most beautiful poetry in the book of Psalms. The Psalms were poems that were sung. Some of the things they expressed were praise to God, confession of fear or sin, and thanksgiving.

ex: Psalm 29

Ascribe to the Lord, O sons of the mighty.
Ascribe to the Lord glory and strength,
Ascribe to the Lord the glory due to His name;
Worship the Lord in holy array.

The voice of the Lord is upon the waters;
The god of glory thunders,
The Lord is over many waters.
The voice of the Lord is powerful,
The voice of the Lord is majestic.
The voice of the Lord breaks the cedars;
Yes, the Lord breaks in pieces the cedars of Lebanon.
And He makes Lebanon skip like a calf.
And Sirion like a young wild ox.
The voice of the Lord hews out flames of fire.
The voice of the Lord shakes the wilderness;
The Lord shakes the wilderness of Kadesh.
The voice of the Lord makes the deer to calve,
And strips the forests bare,
And in His temple everything says, "Glory!"

The Lord sat as King at the flood;
Yes, the Lord sits as King forever.
The Lord will give strength to His people;
The Lord will bless His people with peace.

Notice the form of the Psalm. It is written in poetry form. Can you find any similes?

Sometimes the psalmist uses a repetitive word or phrase in a psalm. What words are repeated in Psalm 29? What effect does this have?

Another well known psalm that uses a repeating phrase is Psalm 136 which begins:

Give thanks to the Lord, for He is good;
    For His lovingkindness is everlasting.
Give thanks to the God of gods,
    For His lovingkindness is everlasting.

Give thanks to the Lord of lords,
    For His lovingkindness is everlasting.
To Him Who alone does great wonders,
    For His lovingkindness is everlasting.

This pattern continues throughout the psalm. Do you think it has a pleasing rhythm?

Read a few psalms today. Note any repeating phrases or words.

Day Two

We find many examples of figurative language in the Psalms. Psalm 131 speaks of a childlike trust in the Lord:

O Lord, my heart is not proud, nor my eyes haughty;
Nor do I involve myself in great matters,
Or in things too difficult for me.
Surely I have composed and quieted my soul;
Like a weaned child rests against his mother,
My soul is like a weaned child within me.
O Israel, hope in the Lord
From this time forth and forever.

What does the psalmist compare his soul to?

Psalm 133 speaks of brotherly unity. Notice the rich imagery used.

Behold, how good and how pleasant it is
    for brothers to dwell together in unity!
It is like the precious oil upon the head,
Coming down upon the beard,
    Even Aaron's beard,
Coming down upon the edge of his robes.
It is like the dew of Hermon,
Coming down upon the mountains of Zion;
For there the Lord commanded the blessing
    - life forever.

Read some Psalms today noting simile and metaphor used.

Day Three

The Scripture exhorts us to "...be filled with the Spirit; speaking to yourselves in psalms..." (Eph. 5:18-19). Today you will begin writing a psalm of your own.

You may choose to use a repeating phrase as we read on Day One. You could express your joy in remembering what God has done in the past and your confidence in what He will do in the future. Your psalm could be an expression of gratitude for benefits God has given you such as forgiveness, peace, confidence, protection, provision, and deliverance. Your psalm could express a need or a cry for help in troubled times.

It may also be helpful to use some of the key phrases that David used to express his need for God, such as "I lift up my soul to Thee", "I cry unto Thee," "Thy face, Lord, will I seek".
Find other key phrases as you read through the psalms.

Here is a psalm written by Erin Welch, age 10:

I shall be satisfied when I awake with Thy likeness.
I shall be satisfied when I walk in Thy presence.
I shall be satisfied when Thy face looketh well upon me.

The arm of the Lord is bold and just.
The arm of the Lord made the heavens and the earth.
The earth trembled when the Lord set His foot upon it.
The earth quaked and its mountains smoked when the Lord spoke.

Good and upright is the Lord and worthy of praise.
Let the nations laud Him.
Let the name of the Lord be praised.

I shall praise the Lord on the mountains.
I shall praise the Lord in the valleys.
I shall lift the name of the Lord on high!

Great is the Lord and worthy of honor.
Great is the name of the Lord.
Great is the Lord who is worthy of praise.

I shall enter His courts with thanksgiving in my heart.
I shall enter His courts with praise.
I shall honor the name of my King.
Praise the Lord!

Day Four

You may continue working on your psalm or if you finished one yesterday, try choosing another theme. Read your psalms out loud. You will also enjoy memorizing them.

Day Five

Spend today finishing your writing, reading the Psalms aloud, or reciting your own.

LESSON SIX
Finishing Up

All writers, even poets, go through a process of revising and editing their work. This is hard work, but well worth it. Why should you spend time revising and editing your work? First of all, when you care about what you have written, you want it to be your very best effort. Sometimes, when we are quickly getting our thoughts down on paper or searching for a rhyme, we write down our first thoughts. Later, as we have time to think about what we have written, we find it is not exactly what we meant.

For example, a student was given the assignment to write a poem modeled after Irene Rutherford McLeod's poem "Lone Dog". She chose to write about a deer, beginning:

I'm a sleek deer, a meek deer, a fast deer and brown.
I'm a shy deer, a spry deer, pounding o'er the ground.

When she came to the third line, she needed another internal rhyme and came up with:

I'm a hasty deer, a tasty deer, running all the day.
I love to jump and leap on logs, and watch the little
         fawns play.

When we discussed the poem we both decided that while "a hasty deer, a tasty deer" was a good rhyme, it didn't exactly convey the idea she had in mind. It made you think of eating the deer. She got out a synonym finder and revised her poem to read:

I'm a running deer, a cunning deer, running all the day.

You cannot hope to improve your writing if you think it cannot be changed once it is written down.

It can be very difficult to read your own work with an objective eye. Since writing is such hard work, we tend to become very attached to what we have written. You may find it helpful to talk over your work with your teacher. Some questions you can discuss are:

Have I really said what I meant to say?
Have I chosen words that express my intent clearly?
How can my work be improved?

Choose one of the poems you have written. Read it aloud. Does it need some revision to make it better? Read it aloud to your teacher. Discuss the poem. Make any changes you feel will improve the poem. For example, you may want to change, add, or drop a word or line.

Day Two   Editing

Editing your work is not as hard as revising. Part of editing is making sure you have no grammar, spelling, or punctuation errors. This will require a lot of concentration and care about details. You may want to proofread several times. Again, your teacher will be able to help you, but try to proofread your work first and catch as many errors as you can before you ask for your teacher's help.

Proofread some of your work looking for any grammar, spelling, or punctuation errors. A grammar book and a dictionary will be useful for reference.

Day Three

Continue revising and editing the poems you have written during this unit. Begin making a neat copy of your completed work.

Take the time today to review the lessons in this unit. Answer the following questions:

What is a simile?
What is a metaphor?
What is personification?
Give an example of each.
What three things make up the metrical pattern of a poem?
Define feet.
What is the importance of revisions?
What does editing entail?

Day Five

Finish the unit by reading aloud and discussing your poems and any other poems of your choice, or make a booklet containing your poems. You may wish to illustrate them.

WRITING A RESEARCH PAPER
A Three-Week Unit

Week One

Sometimes you need to write a research paper for history or science or maybe just to learn more about a topic that interests you. In this unit you will learn how to choose a topic about which you are interested in learning more. The topic you choose to write about in this unit should do one of two things. One may be to inform your reader. This is called a factual research paper. You may choose to write a problem-centered research paper, a research project for a science fair competition, or a topic of interest.

A checklist is provided for you on page 59 to help you keep track of your progress.

Begin by choosing a general area of interest and then try narrowing it down to a more limited topic. It is difficult to handle research if your topic is too broad. For example:

General area of interest: Fungi
General topic: Mold
Limited topic: The History of Penicillin

You may find as you begin gathering information that the emphasis may shift or you will have to refine the wording of your topic.

If you have trouble finding a topic, it might help you to create a semantic map. Think of all the words you can that relate to any given subject. Allow your mind to make associations. This will help you to narrow your subject and may also help you think of a topic you had not considered before.

After you have decided on the topic of your paper, you should spend some time in the library. Begin by looking up information about your general topic in the library's card catalog, periodicals, and major encyclopedias. Do not rely on just one source. Try to find as many varied sources as you can. If you cannot find what you need ask the librarian to help you.

Day Two   Bibliography

Use today's time becoming acquainted with your sources. You may find after scanning the books or articles you have checked out, that some will not be useful to you.

After you have collected your sources you will want to compile a bibliography. If you keep track of your sources during the research process, it will make writing the final bibliography much easier. These entries may be recorded on index cards. Include the following facts:

1. Author (or editor)
2. Title (of book or article)
3. Publication facts
    a. books: city, publisher, date
    b. encyclopedias: name, year
    c. periodicals: title, volume or number, date, pages

You may also wish to include the library call number in case you need to find the source again.

Day Three: Taking Notes

Before you begin your research, you might find it helpful to write down questions you would like to answer or thoughts about your topic. Arrange the questions or thoughts into common groups, and give a heading to these groups. This will act as an outline for you to follow as you collect information. Now you are ready to begin taking notes.

You will need 3 x 5 cards and a case to keep them in. As you read, write down facts or ideas on these cards. Using your outline, write a heading on each note card. Put information from one book on a notecard, indicating the author and title (you may need this for footnotes or to re-check information). Summarize the information in your own words. If you must copy something, put quotation marks around it and indicate the source and page number where the quotation can be found. It is best to write a single piece of information on each card. This will make it easier for you to arrange the cards in whatever order fits your paper.

Day Four

Continue taking notes.

Day Five

Continue taking notes.

LESSON TWO
First Draft

Organize your note cards by headings. You may find you need to collect more data or revise your topic. Using just your notes and your outline, you are ready to begin writing. Keep in mind that you are writing the first draft of your paper, not the final copy.

Begin by writing an introductory paragraph. This will introduce your topic and should capture the attention of your reader. To do this, you might include a quote, a brief anecdote, a question, or a striking fact.

Using your outline, write the middle paragraphs of your paper. Write a good topic sentence for each subpoint of your outline. Cover each of the subpoints of the outline using transitions such as <u>however</u>, <u>also</u>, <u>then</u>, <u>next</u> to connect the paragraphs.

Finally, you need to write a concluding paragraph summing up the main ideas of your paper. Again, you might choose to use a quote or an anecdote to sum up the thrust of the paper.

After you have completed your first draft, go back and read what you have written, making any revisions you think necessary.
Use a different color pen when you correct something. This makes it easier to identify changes.

Ask the following questions:

1. Is there a paragraph for each subtopic of my outline?
2. Does the information in each paragraph relate to its topic sentence?
3. Are the introductory paragraph and concluding paragraph interesting?
4. Are there valid transitions from one point to another?

This is also the time to carefully check spelling, grammar, punctuation, and sentence and paragraph structure. You will find a thesaurus helpful in changing any words that you have repeated too often or in finding a more effective word.

LESSON THREE
Final Draft

Let your teacher read your first draft. As you discuss the paper, make note of any comments or changes needed. Make any necessary changes. If possible, type your paper.

Your paper should include a Title Page containing the title of your paper, your name, and the date. The Bibliography should come after the body of the paper. Arrange the items alphabetically by author. Do not indent the first line of the Bibliography entry, but do indent the following lines.

The general format for a book reference is:

Author's name (last name first), <u>Title</u> (underlined), book edition
(if indicated), place of publication, publisher's name in
full, year of publication.

The general format for a periodical (magazine) is:

Author's name (last name first), "Title of Article" (in quotation
marks), <u>Name of Magazine</u> (underlined), date of publication,
page reference.

Here is how to list articles in reference works:

<u>The World Book Encyclopedia</u>, 1990 ed. S.V. "Automobiles", by John Smith.

(S.V. indicates the subject under which you should look.)

When you have finished, carefully proofread your paper looking for any final corrections that may need to be made. After all corrections have been made, place your paper neatly in a cover.

STUDENT CHECKLIST

Choose a Subject - - - - - - - - ☐

Narrow the Subject - - - - - - - - ☐

Select Research Materials - - - - - - - ☐

Formulate Bibliography - - - - - - - - ☐

Write an Outline - - - - - - - - ☐

Prepare Note Cards and Take Notes - - - - - - ☐

Write First Draft - - - - - - - - ☐

Revise First Draft - - - - - - - ☐

Write Final Copy - - - - - - - ☐

SPEECH
A Three-Week Unit

This unit will not be presented on a day by day assignment basis. You will be given instructions for the week and will need to pace yourself.

Week One   **Choosing a Subject**

In real life people speak to specific groups for specific reasons. Your reasons for giving a speech might be to present something you learned to your family or friends or a report to your homeschool co-op group. Do not choose something you think is boring. Your audience will find it boring, too. You can choose a topic that will inform, amuse, or persuade. You can talk about interesting experiences you have had, places you have been, a person you know, or something interesting you have learned. Do not try to cover too much territory.

Make a list of three subjects you think you can talk about and discuss them with your teacher. This will help you choose the best one. Try to come up with an interest-grabbing title. After you have decided on the subject, you will need to define the purpose of your speech. Do you wish to entertain, inform, or persuade your audience? For example, if the subject you have chosen is skateboarding, your purpose could be to entertain by relating some of your mishaps learning to ride a skateboard. If your purpose is to inform, you would talk about the equipment involved and different stunts or techniques used in skateboarding. Or you may choose to persuade your audience that skateboarding is a safe, healthy sport.

Go back to your list of three possible subjects and see if you can find three different purposes for speaking about it.

After you have decided what you are going to talk about and why you are going to talk about it, then you need to think about how you are going to arrange your talk. If you plan to tell a story or describe a process, you will tell what happened first, what happened second, etc. If you are trying to persuade, you could arrange your speech by stating a problem and telling what to do about it or asking a question and then answering it. Your topic may just follow logical divisions.

You are now ready to do some research, if needed, about your topic. Review the research techniques taught in the Research Paper Unit.

Week Two   The First Draft

You will spend this week finishing your research and note taking and begin writing your speech. Decide how you want to organize your speech and write a brief outline listing main points with their subpoints underneath.

Although you will not be reading or memorizing your speech word for word, you will need to write out the speech. After you have your speech outlined, you are ready to begin writing your first draft. You will want to begin with a good opening sentence or two to capture your audience's attention.

Four possible openings are by asking a question, using a quotation, telling a short relevant story or saying something funny to introduce your subject.

Next you should tell where you are going and how you plan to get there by stating the title or subject of your talk and briefly stating your main points.

The body of your speech will consist of your first main point and the supporting subpoints, the second main point and material supporting the point and so on.

The last main section of your speech is the conclusion. Here you will either sum up what you have said, make a final appeal, or open the floor for questions, if appropriate.

Week Three   Final Revision, Practice, Presentation

You should be ready to edit your first draft now. Read your speech aloud to make sure it is not too long or too short. How is the flow or continuity? Did you use good connecting words? Did you use the word "I" too many times? Is the grammar correct? Read your draft several times focusing on each of these questions. Make the necessary corrections.

You are ready to practice presenting your speech. Remember, you are not trying to memorize your speech word for word, but you need to be very familiar with your material. The best way to do this is to practice your speech in your room all by yourself. Do this several times. Now you are ready to practice saying it to your teacher or a friend until you are very comfortable with it.

After this practice you will be ready for the final presentation. You may use your outline, or make simple notes on note cards to refer to during the speech. Make sure you are dressed neatly; first impressions are important!

Some final suggestions:

If you are seated facing your audience before you are introduced:

DO NOT tilt your chair back.
DO NOT gaze at the ceiling.
DO NOT yawn.
DO NOT wave to people you know in the audience.
DO NOT whisper to people sitting by you.

When you begin speaking:

DO stand up straight.
DO look at your audience.
DO keep your feet fairly close together with your weight
    on both feet.
DO speak clearly and project your voice.
DO use gestures to stress a point.
DO NOT lean on the podium.
DO NOT play with anything in your hands.

THE SHORT STORY
A Six-Week Unit

Holidays, house guests, or illness may require a shorter unit occasionally. This unit can be divided into three two-part units making it easier to accommodate your schedule.

These 3 two-week units will be spent writing short stories. This should be a somewhat more relaxed time for you and a fun time to use your imagination.

General Guidelines:

There are three main aspects of a short story: setting, characters, and plot.

When you write a story you have to imagine where the characters are. The setting of the story tells when and where the story takes place. You may tell when your story takes place by mentioning a specific date or using words that help your reader guess what general time period the story is set in. The setting is important because very often it affects what the characters do. It can also set the mood for the story.

Along with the setting you must develop your characters well in order to have a good story. If you tell what a character looks like and describe his mannerisms, then your readers begin to feel they know him. The character's reactions to different situations give your readers more insight into that character's feelings and thoughts.

What the character says, the dialogue, gives the reader further information. Without using dialogue, you are just narrating your story. You can tell the story quicker this way, but it will not be as interesting. Conversation makes you feel as if you are listening to the characters and are part of the story. The setting and description of the characters can be revealed through dialogue.

The plot of the story tells the action. There are four general steps to develop the plot of the story: introduction, conflict, climax, and resolution.

The introduction defines the setting and the mood and introduces the main characters.

A conflict is a problem the main character has to deal with. There is usually one major complication, but there you may develop several smaller ones as the story progresses. These create tension and hold the reader's interest. The conflict faced may be an internal conflict (such as shyness) or an external conflict (such as solving a mystery).

The climax is the turning point of the story and should be the most exciting part.

The resolution finishes the story, tying up all the loose ends.

Check List

1. Have you chosen an interesting title?
2. Is your setting clear?
3. Do your characters fit in the setting?
4. Does your dialogue match your characters? Is it believable?
5. Is your plot clear?
6. Do the events of your story follow a logical pattern?
7. Do you resolve the conflict?

A suggested schedule for the 3 two-week units is:

Unit One: Historical Fiction

Set your story some time in history. For example: the Civil War period or Columbus' voyage to America.

Unit Two: Current Fiction

Set this story in the present. Choose some place you are very familiar with as the setting of your story.

Unit Three: Fanciful Fiction

Assign personalities to inanimate objects (tools, food, etc.) or make animals talk in this fun story.

STAR OF LIGHT
A Four Week Unit

Lesson One (Chapters l-6)

Day One

The book you will be reading and studying during this unit is <u>Star</u> <u>of</u> <u>Light</u>. The author, Patricia St. John, is an English missionary and has written many books about children. Read the Introductory Note. Look at a map and find out where this story might have taken place.

Read Chapters l-3

Compare and contrast the way women, children, and marriage are treated in Hamid's country to ways they are treated in our country.

Research blindness. Read a biography of Helen Keller, Fanny Crosby, and/or Louis Braille.

Day Two

Listen carefully as your teacher reads Chapters 4 - 6 out loud. After your teacher has read these chapters, try retelling this portion of the story in your own words. This is called narration.

Day Three

Chapters l-6 introduced Hamid, his sister Kinza, their mother, and their stepfather. During the next three days you will be writing a "character sketch" of these main characters. This means you will be writing a short paper describing the character. Write in the first person as if you were the character. Today, write from Hamid's point of view. Tell how he feels about his sister and family and their situation. Tell of his problems and concerns as if you were Hamid.

Day Four

Today, you will write a "character sketch" of Kinza. Tell how she feels about her family and situation. Write as if you were Kinza describing her blindness and how she "sees" her world.

Day Five

How would you feel if you were Hamid's mother? Describe her life as if you were her. Finally, and this might be the hardest to do, create a "character sketch" of Hamid's stepfather. How do you think he thinks and feels?

Lesson Two (Chapters 7-12)

Day One

Listen carefully as your teacher reads Chapter 7 "A Narrow Escape". Narrate the chapter back to her with as much detail as you remember.

Day Two

Read Chapters 8 and 9

Draw an imaginary map of Hamid and Kinza's journey. Include the places mentioned and label them.

Day Three

Read Chapters 10-12 silently.

Read Chapter 11 out loud to your teacher. Use good expression and speak clearly.

Day Four

What is an analogy? Can you think of some examples? In the chapter "Two Broken Eggs", the English nurse makes an analogy about walking in the light and being clean to help teach Hamid an important spiritual truth. Today you will begin writing an analogy. Write about something that has happened to you or someone you know that illustrates a spiritual lesson.

Day Five

Complete writing the analogy you began yesterday.

Lesson Three (Chapters 13-17)

Day One

Read Chapters 13 and 14

A new character has been introduced, Jenny Swift. Write a character sketch of Jenny as you did of the other main characters during Week One.

Day Two

Draw a map showing the probable route taken by Jenny and her family from England to North Africa.

Day Three

Read Chapters 15-17

Discuss Jenny's statement at the end of Chapter 16: "If only Kinza could come back," said Jenny to herself. "I would never be disobedient or naughty again. I'd be good for ever and ever."

Day Four

Research the Islam religion.

Day Five

Write a paper contrasting Islam and Christianity. Did Mohammed claim to be God? Did he perform miracles? How is the question of sin handled? What about eternity? How do each teach we are to live?

Lesson Four (Chapters 18-22)

Day One

Listen as your teacher reads Chapter 18 "A Daring Plan". Narrate back to her what you remember. Include as much detail as possible.

Day Two

Before reading the last four chapters, discuss with your teacher what you think will happen to Hamid, Kinza, and Jenny. How would you end the story?

Read Chapters 19-22

Day Three

Who was the main character in the first part of the book? Who was the main character in the second part of the book? Each of these characters changed as the story was told. Write a paragraph for each character describing the ways in which they changed.

Day Four

Write a synopsis of the book. Tell the main events in order and include a paragraph telling how you liked the book and why.

Day Five

Complete your synopsis today. Make a neat copy and place it in a folder with a decorated cover.

ADAM AND HIS KIN
A Four Week Unit

The book you will read and base your research and writing on during this four week unit is <u>Adam and His Kin</u> by Dr. Ruth Beechick. This book is a simple narrative of the first eleven chapters of Genesis. In addition to the Bible, Dr. Beechick has gathered her information from many sources including astronomy, archeology, and ancient traditions and religions.

First, read Genesis chapters 1 - 11 from Appendix B of the book, and then read <u>Adam and His Kin</u>. Now you are ready to begin your research and writing assignments. Read through the four activities given below. There is no "right" order to work through these activities.

<u>Adam and His Kin</u> Activities

1.   Your Choice

Reading <u>Adam and His Kin</u> may have given you a fresh look at the first eleven chapters of Genesis. Maybe it answered some questions you had or made you think of new questions. Write out some questions you still don't know the answers to. Take the time to do some independent research to try to find some of the answers. Begin by discussing your questions with your parents. You might set up an appointment with your pastor to ask him the questions. Next, stop by the church library to look for books and commentaries that might help. Write a report about one or more of the topics you looked into.

2.   Origins

As Christians we believe that the world and all it contains was created by God.

In the beginning God created the heavens and the earth.
Genesis 1:1

Ah, Lord God, behold You have made the heavens and the earth by your great power and outstretched arm! Nothing is too hard for you.

Jeremiah 32:17

Lord, You are God who made heaven and earth and the sea, and all that is in them...

Acts 4:24

Read one or more books by authors who defend this creationist view. Some books are suggested below. If these seem difficult to read, try scanning the tables of contents to find chapters that have the information you are looking for.

The Genesis Record, The Biblical Basis for Modern Science, The Bible has the Answer, all by Dr. Henry M. Morris

The Controversy - Roots of the Creation-Evolution Conflict by Donald E. Chittick

Unlocking the Mysteries of Creation by Dennis R. Petersen
or any other appropriate books.

Talk to your parents about what you are reading. Do they agree with what the books say? Interview your pastor. What has he found in his studies? Maybe you know other grownups who would like to talk about these topics. If you talk to an evolutionist, find out what you can about his beliefs.

Write a theme explaining the evolutionary belief and the creationist belief. This could be a large assignment, but try to summarize a few points about each view, and mention a few of the major problems. Write a concluding paragraph stating your belief and why you think the way you do.

In addition to or instead of the theme on evolution versus creation, you could write about two kinds of creationists. One kind, like the authors listed above, believe in a young earth. That means that God created the earth only a few thousand years ago -- maybe about 6000 years, or not more than 10,000 years ago. The other kind believes in an old earth -- that God created the earth millions of years ago. If you talk to or read an old earth creationist, learn what you can about his or her beliefs. Then write a theme describing the differences between the young earth and the old earth views. Again, write a concluding paragraph stating your belief and why you think the way you do. In both themes it will be all right to state that you're not sure yet of your beliefs, that you want to read and study more before you make up your mind.

> But sanctify the Lord God in your hearts: and be ready always to give an answer to every man that asketh you a reason of the hope that is in you with meekness and fear.
>
> I Peter 3:15

Writing a Theme

The most common form of development of a theme is the deductive, where you have two or three items to discuss which deal with your main idea. The first paragraph will contain a generalization (the thesis statement) of the items. In this case the statement will tell the two views you will be reporting on. For example:

"There are two major views held about the origin of life."

The thesis statement will then be put into an opening paragraph:

"How did life begin? This is a question that most people attempt to answer at some time. There are two major views held about the origin of life. I believe it is important to understand these views in order to better answer this question."

Your next two paragraphs will go on to describe both of the views, what is believed and any major problems with the view. Finally, the last paragraph should contain your conclusion and why you have come to it.

Here are some suggestions to help you through the writing process:

A.   Begin the theme by

-        Asking a question and then stating that you intend to answer it.

-        Using a pertinent quotation from a book, an authority, etc.

- Stating your topic.

- Beginning with a dependent clause: When you think about it...Although most people don't know...

B. Connect the parts

- When similar points are being made use word and phrase connectives: While...moreover...to sum up...furthermore

- When contrasting points are being made use word and phrase connectives: nonetheless... despite this... on the other hand...however

- To indicate stages in your argument use initially...at the onset...to begin with...in condition...lastly...finally

- Number your division: the first...a second...in the third place

- Use parallel sentence structure:

  The Bible explains God's relationship to man.
  The Bible explains man's relationship to God.
  The Bible explains man's relationship to man.

C. End the theme

- with a question.

- with a pertinent question.

- by repeating your opening topic.

- with a personal opinion, additional information, a warning, or a declaration of intent

D.   Proofread

-    Title - Capitalize main words

-    Format - neatness, margins, etc.

-    Check spelling

-    Check for complete sentences

-    Check for problem words: its-it's, whose-who's, theirs-there's, accept-except, affect-effect, to-too, lose-loose, chose-choose

4.   Narration

Compare a chapter in <u>Adam and His Kin</u> with its Biblical reference in Genesis. Notice how closely Dr. Beechick follows the Biblical account. What does she add? How is her writing different? Dr. Beechick is relating the Genesis account in "story form". This is called narration.

<u>Adam and His Kin</u> tells the story through Genesis 11. Read Genesis 12. Following Dr. Beechick's style, try writing the next chapter using what you have just read in Genesis 12. You may use just the Bible or you might like to try drawing some additional information from another source, such as a Christian history book. For example, you could look up Egypt and find out what it was like during this time to help you describe the scene better.

If you enjoy this exercise, narrate the next chapter of Genesis or choose another portion of the Bible to narrate.

5.   Graphs

It has been said that a picture is worth a thousand words. As a researcher and writer you will find there will be times when it will be more helpful to present your information in picture form. A graph is a picture used to present facts so that they will be clearer and easier to understand. It is usually easier to draw conclusions or make comparisons from items illustrated in a graph than to try to figure out columns of figures or paragraphs of facts.

A line graph is one of the simplest types of graphs. The line shows the relationship between two variables or parameters. For example, it can be used to show how man's life expectancy changed from the time of Adam to the time of Abraham.

Referring back to Genesis 5, 9:29, 11, 25:7, 35:28, and 47:28, make a list of all the men mentioned. Next to each man's name record his age at death. Your list should include 22 men from Adam through Abraham. With the data tabulated in this form you may observe some trends.

Now on a sheet of graph paper, or quadrille ruled paper (4 squares to the inch), lay out horizontal (x) and vertical (y) axes for your line graph. The scale of your x and y axes will determine how large your chart is. If you allowed 1/2" spacing for each of the 22 men, your chart would fill up the entire 11" of the page and you wouldn't have room for the rest of the chart. Therefore use 1/4" spacing for each man's name (or whatever is convenient on your graph paper). The names of the men should go on the x axes, along the bottom. You will need to turn the names vertical under the axes to fit them in the 1/4" spacing.

Observing that the oldest man lived 969 years, you may want to mark off your y axis from 0 to 1000 years. Mark off every 100 years using 1/2" spacing for each 100 years. Label this axis "AGE AT DEATH."

Now that you have created your chart axes, put a small dot or an "x" above each man's name, at the location corresponding to his age at death, and connect the dots (or x's) with a line. Your chart is complete except for any titles or explanations you may wish to add.

Trends that you may have noticed before in the tabulated data should be more pronounced using the line graph.

A bar graph also can be used to illustrate trends in data. A bar graph uses vertical or horizontal bars to make comparisons. Prepare your graph as you did for the line graph. Instead of dots or x's marking each man's age, draw a rectangle, or "bar", that extends from the x axis to the point marking the man's age at death.

A horizontal bar graph could also be created by exchanging x and y axes. Starting on the y axis, with Adam at the top, list the 22 men. The x axis would then be marked off for 1000 years. Drawing the bars from left to right gives you a horizontal bar graph.

Another interesting study is how the lives of the earliest humans overlapped. Did you know that Noah's grandfather, Methuselah could have known Adam for over 200 years! You can show this information by making a time line. You've already created a table of ages for the 22 Bible characters. On this same table add each man's age when his son was born.

Create a larger graph area by taping three sheets of graph paper together end-to-end so that the grid spacing is maintained from sheet to sheet. Turn your paper sideways, draw a line 30" long 1" from the bottom. Mark this line for 3000 years, with each inch representing 100 years. On the left hand side of the sheet list the 22 men, with Adam at the bottom.

Now draw a line, or a bar (your choice), next to Adam's name, extending from his time of birth to his death. This line should extend from 1 to 930. From Genesis 5:3, you can see that Seth's line should begin at 130, and verse 8 tells you how long to make it. Calculate birth dates and ages for each of the other men and mark your chart accordingly. Shem and Abram are not so easy to figure as the others. Here are verses to help you. Shem: Genesis 7:6 and 11:10 contain information for figuring when Shem was born. Abram: Genesis 11:32 and 12:4, along with Acts 7:4, contain information for figuring the age of Terah when Abram was born. Abram was much younger than his brother Haran.

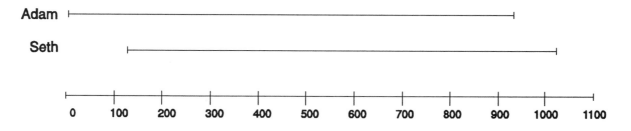

You now have a time line which starts with the year 0 at the creation of the world. But what year was that using our present dating system? A good Bible handbook, dictionary, or atlas will give you an approximate date for Abraham. You can then write dates relative to our system under your original dates.

One last type of graph you can work with is the family tree. Look at the family trees Dr. Beechick worked out for you in Adam and His Kin on pages 43 and 61. These family trees basically follow one line of descendants. Draw a family tree, either for your family, by asking your parents, grandparents, aunts and uncles for information; or for someone else that you know by interviewing their family members.

Teacher Helps
Diagramming Sentences

Lesson One
Day One

Nouns Pronouns and Verbs

Noun	Verb
rest	was
we	reached
we	were taken
coachman	made

Day Two

Diagramming the Simple Verb
and Simple Subject of the Verb

rest	was

we	were taken

we	reached

coachman	made

Day Three

Adjectives

Adjective	Noun Modifier
A huge tawny	mastiff
This great	creature
The little	fellow

Day Four

Lesson Two
Day One

Adverbs

Adverb	Verb Modifier
almost	seemed
not	could stop
feebly	waved
then	fainted

Day Two

Diagramming Adverbs

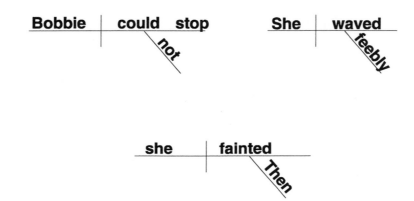

Day Three

Direct Objects and Indirect Objects

advised	him	(D.O.)
bought	me	(D.O.)
hired	stable	(D.O.)
engaged	man	(D.O.)

brought   Jerry   (I.O)   basin (D.O.)

Lesson Two
Day Four

Diagramming Direct Objects
and Indirect Objects

| doctor | advised | him |

| he | bought | me |

| He | hired | stable |

| He | engaged | man |

| Dolly | had brought | basin |

  \ Jerry

Lesson Three
Day One

Predicate Adjectives
and Predicate Nouns

Jeremiah Barker	PN
match	PN
plump	PA
tall	PA
lad	PN

Day Two
Diagramming Predicate Adjectives
and Predicate Nouns

| wife | was \ match |

| she | was \ plump |

| boy | was \ tall |

| He | was \ lad |

Lesson Three
Day Three

Qualifiers

quite   (accidentally)
very   (earnestly)
rather   (odd)
very   (often)
somewhat   (different)

Note: really - adverb

Day Four

Diagramming Qualifiers

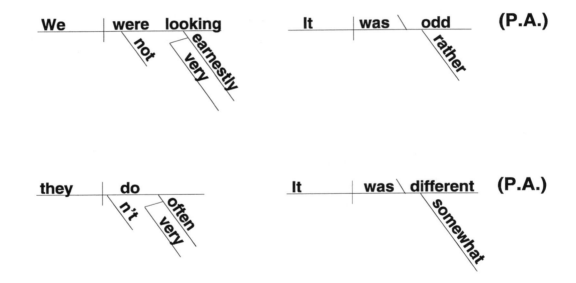

Lesson Four
Day One

Prepositional Phrases - Part 1

into the mistress' low chaise
to us
to us
on Ginger
across the country

Lesson Four
Day Two

Prepositional Phrases - Part 2

at her wits' end	adjective
into the parlor	adverb
as a sort	adverb
of sacred place	adjective (modifies "sort")
over all the chairs	adverb
for fear	adverb
of flies	adjective (modifies "fear")

Day Three

Diagramming Prepositional Phrases

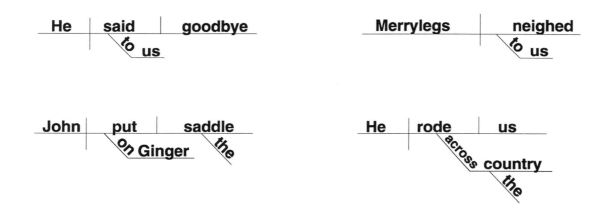

Lesson Four
Day Five

Interjections

Oh
Yes
Right
Please
Sure
Hello

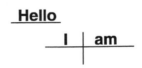

Lesson Five
Day One

Conjunctions

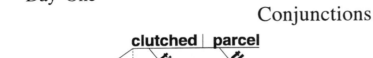

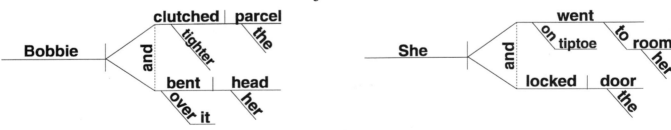

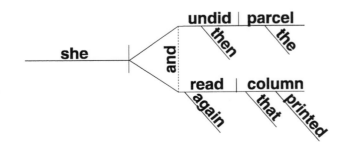

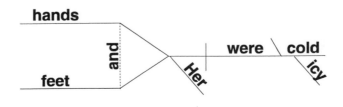

Lesson Five
Day Two

Compound Modifiers, Compound Object of the Preposition Compound Direct Objects

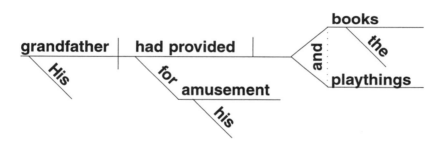

Day Three

Compound Phrases

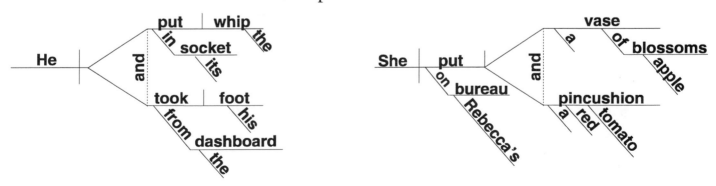

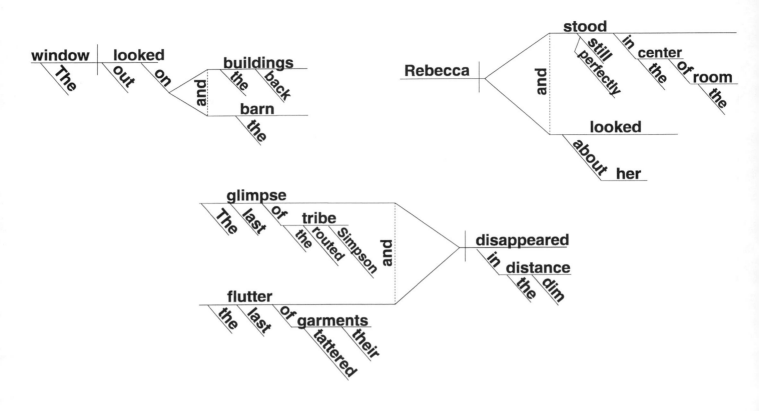

Day Four

Compound Sentences

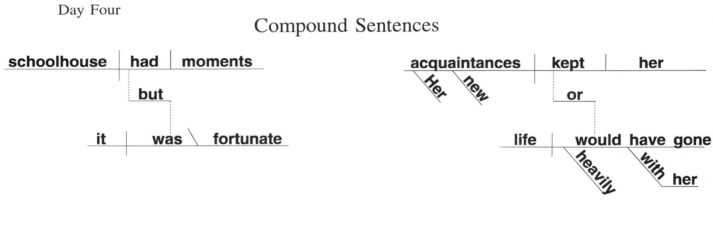

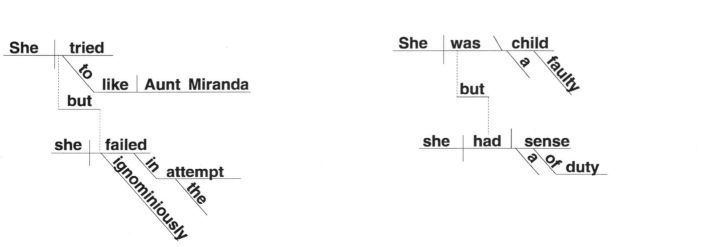

Lesson Six
Day One

Gerunds and Gerund Phrases

Blessings
Keeping
getting
churning
churning
teaching
understanding
teaching

Day Two

Participles and Participial Phrases

weeping	wife
loving	words
roaring	waters
refreshing	milk
damaged	biscuits
loving	care
rushing	noise
broken	eggshells

Day Three

Infinitives and Infinitive Phrases

to keep my countenance
to cook so many at once
to preserve them
to go for her cask after dinner
to load
to leave

Lesson Six
Day Four

Review Parts of Sentence

        part. prep. adj. adj.   adj.   O.P. subj. verb   inf.   conj. inf. prep   O.P.
Turning up his little wrinkled face, Jocko began to grimace and beg for something.

adj. subj. verb   adj. D.O. conj. verb prep adj. adj. D.O. Prep adj. O.P.   adj.   subj.   verb   adv.
The man pulled the string and struck up a merry tune. In a minute the monkey spun around

conj.   adv.   prep adj adj.   O.P. conj. verb prep adj.   adj.   O.P.   adj.   adj. subj.   verb   adv.
and around at a lively pace and put in many queer antics. The little audience was fairly

     verb   prep   O.P.
convulsed with laughter.

(adapted from <u>Five Little Peppers and How They Grew</u> by Margaret Sidney)

Day Five

Review Sentence Diagramming

Poetry

Lesson Two
Day One

little flames aspire like small decrepit souls

Day Two

The rain pitter-pattered on the roof like tiny feet.
The wind whispered in the trees like a lullabye.
The cat stalked on the fence like a prowler.
The light glistened on the water like diamonds.

soft as a feather
cute as a baby
cold as winter
brave as a soldier
white as fresh snow

Day Three

Grace is a plant.

Her heart is a garden. (metaphor)
Her heart, a garden, quaint and sweet (implied metaphor)

The morns are meeker.
The berry's cheek is plumper.
The maple wears a gayer scarf.
The field a scarlet gown.

Possible answers:
> made noise (groaned)
> flew by (danced through the air)
> fell (leaped)
> came (peeked)

Lesson Four
Day Two

Trochaic	a a b b c c	

Day Three

Iambic	a b a b	1st stanza
	a b c b	2nd - 4th stanza

Day Four

Iambic	a a a b	1st stanza
	c c c b	2nd stanza

Lesson Five
Day One

Similes: Lebanon skip like a calf
Sirion like a young wild ox

Ascribe to the Lord.
The voice of the Lord.
The repitition creates rhythm and shows emphasis.

Day Two

He compares his soul to a weaned child.

Bible Character	Age At Death	Age At Son's Birth	Birth Date	Death Date
Adam	930	130	0	930
Seth	912	105	130	1042
Enos	905	90	235	1140
Cainan	910	70	325	1235
Mahalaleel	895	65	395	1290
Jared	962	162	460	1422
Enoch	365	65	622	987
Methuselah	969	187	687	1656
Lamech	777	182	874	1651
Noah	950	500	1056	2006
Shem	600	100	1556	2158
Arphaxad	438	35	1658	2096
Salah	433	30	1693	2126
Eber	464	34	1723	2187
Peleg	239	30	1757	1996
Reu	239	32	1787	2026
Serug	230	30	1819	2049
Nahor	148	29	1849	1997
Terah	205	130	1878	2083
Abraham	175	100	2008	2183
Isaac	180	60	2108	2288
Jacob	147		2168	2315

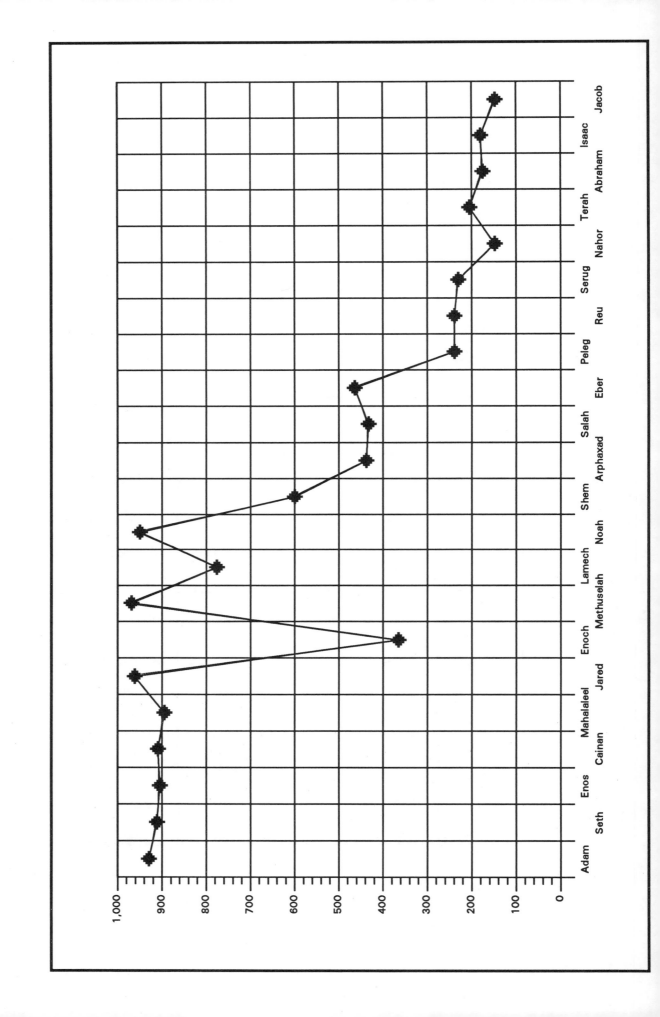

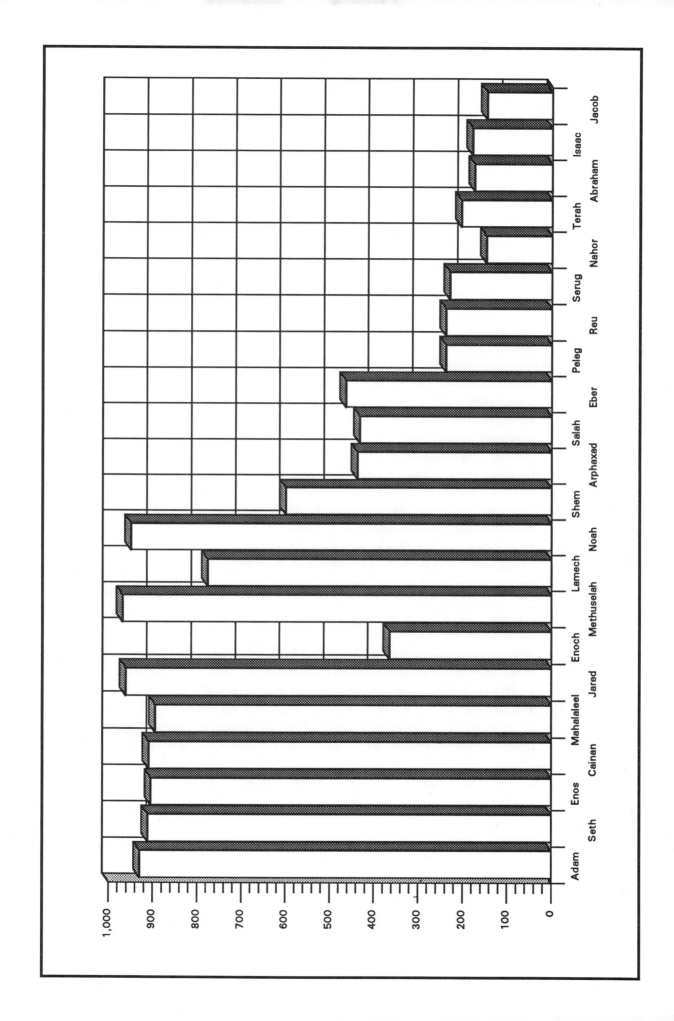

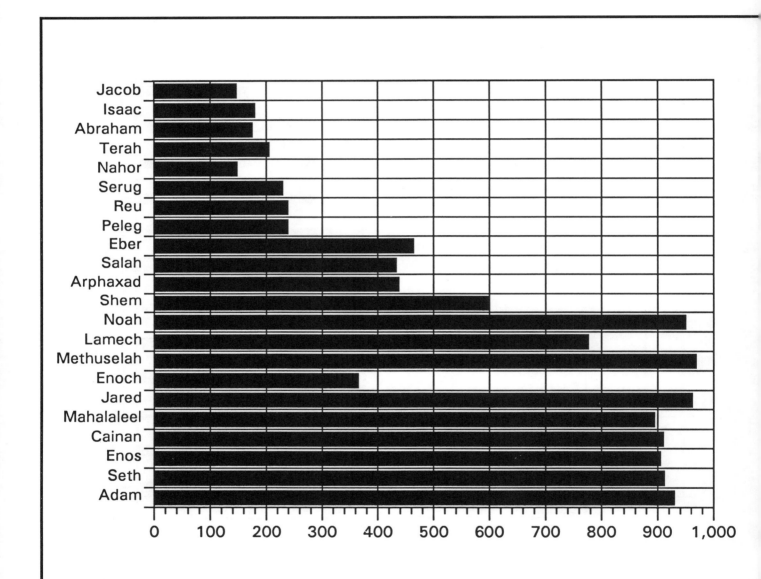

YEARS OF THE PATRIARCHS

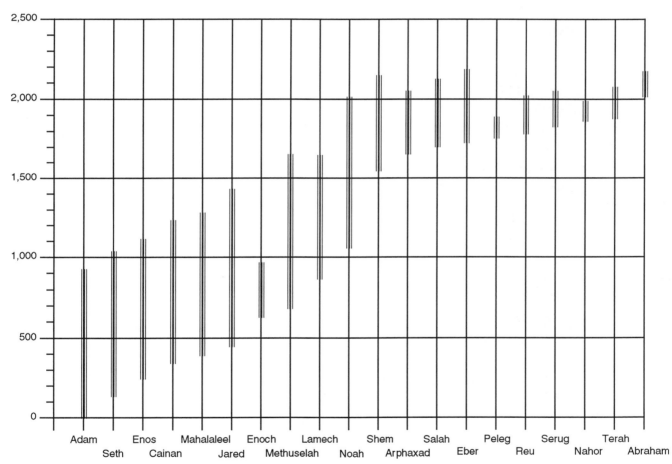

SKILLS INDEX

Unit One - Parts of Speech/Sentence Diagramming

Adjectives
Adverbs
Articles
Compound Direct Objects
Compound Modifiers
Compound Object of the Preposition
Compound Phrases
Compound Sentences
Compound Verb
Conjunctions
Determiners
Direct Objects
Gerunds
Gerund Phrases
Indirect Objects
Infinitives
Infinitive Phrases
Interjections
Nouns
Participial Phrases
Participles
Possessives
Predicate Adjectives
Predicate Nouns
Prepositional Phrases
Prepositions
Pronouns
Qualifiers
Verbs

Unit Two - Poetry

Appreciation
Cinquain
Cliches
Diamante
Editing
Free Verse
Haiku
Imagery
Implied metaphor
Limerick
Metaphor
Meter
Memorization
Personification
Psalms
Recitation
Revision
Rhyme Scheme
Simile
Structural Poems
Writing

Unit Three - Writing a Research Paper

Bibliography
Choosing the Topic
Final Draft
First Draft
Student Checklist
Taking Notes

Unit Four - Speech

Choosing a Subject
Entertainment
Information
Final Revision
First Draft
Persuasion
Practice
Presentation

Unit Five - The Short Story

Characters
Climax
Conflict
Current Fiction
Dialogue
Fanciful Fiction
Historical Fiction
Plot
Resolution
Setting

Unit Six - <u>Star of Light</u>

Analogies
Book Report (Synopsis)
Character Sketches
Comparison
Critical Thinking
Illustrating
Map Skills
Narration
Reading Aloud
Reading Comprehension
Research

Unit Seven - <u>Adam and His Kin</u>

Bar Graphs
Comparison
Family Trees
Interviewing
Line Graphs
Narration
Persuasive Arguments
Reading Comprehension
Reporting
Research
Time Lines
Writing a Theme

BIBLIOGRAPHY

Adam and His Kin. Ruth Beechick. 1990. Arrow Press.

The Bible Has the Answers. Henry Morris. 1971. Baker Books.

The Biblical Basis for Modern Science. Henry Morris. 1984 Baker Books.

Black Beauty. Anna Sewell. 1877.

The Controversy - Roots of the Creation-Evolution Conflict. Donald E. Chittick.
    1984.

Five Little Peppers and How They Grew. Margaret Sydney. 1881.

The Genesis Record. Henry Morris. Baker Books.

Little Lord Fauntleroy. Francis Hodgson Burnett. 1886.

The Railway Children. E. Nesbit. 1906.

Rebecca of Sunnybrook Farm. Kate Douglas Wiggin. 1903.

Star of Light. Patricia St. John. 1953. Moody Press.

Swiss Family Robinson. Johann Wyss. 1813.

Unlocking the Mysteries of Creation. Dennis R. Petersen. 1986. Multnomal
    Press.